LIGHTNING BOLT BOOKS™

How Can I Be a Good Digital Citizen?

Christine Zuchora-Walske

Lerner Publications • Minneapolis

Content Consultant: John Sartori, Assistant Professor, Electrical and Computer Engineering,
University of Minnesota

Lerner Publications Company
A division of Lerner Publishing Group, Inc.
241 First Avenue North
Minneapolis, MN 55401 USA

For reading levels and more information, look up this title at www.lernerbooks.com.

Library of Congress Cataloging-in-Publication Data

Zuchora-Walske, Christine.
    How can i be a good digital citizen? / by Christine Zuchora-Walske.
        pages   cm. — (Lightning bolt books. Our digital world)
    Includes index.
    ISBN 978-1-4677-8078-0 (lb : alk. paper) — ISBN 978-1-4677-8311-8 (pb : alk. paper) —
ISBN 978-1-4677-8312-5 (eb pdf)
        1. Internet and children—Juvenile literature. 2. Computers and children—Juvenile
literature. 3. Internet—Safety measures—Juvenile literature. 4. Online etiquette—Juvenile
literature. I. Title.
    HQ784.I58Z83 2016
    004.67'8083—dc23   2015000313

Manufactured in the United States of America
1 – BP – 7/15/15

Table of Contents

A Digital Adventure

Computers are a big part of our lives. Most American homes have a desktop computer, a laptop, a tablet, or a smartphone. Many homes have more than one of these devices.

Smartphones do many of the same things as personal computers, including sending e-mails and playing videos.

Computers let you learn and have fun from the comfort of your home.

Computers are useful. They can help you learn new information. You can explore new places and new ideas with a computer.

Computers can help you be creative. You can write, make videos, or create music with a computer.

You can use a computer to share your creations. You can play games and chat with your friends.

Video chatting programs let people talk to family and friends.

A computer is a doorway to adventure. Real-life adventures are safer and more fun with others. The same is true with adventures online.

Parents can give you tips on safe computer use.

Tell an adult what you'd like to do when using a computer. That way, the adult can help you if you need it.

Choosing Wisely

Computer use can be good for you. Computers can help you learn about things that interest you. You can also use a computer to talk with your friends.

Computers can be great tools for doing homework.

Computer use can also be bad for you. It can hog all your time. It can give you wrong information. It may even put you in danger.

Staying up late using computers can be unhealthful.

You must use computers wisely. That's part of being a good digital citizen. Visit websites and play games that are made for kids your age.

Visiting websites made for kids can help you stay safe online.

Teachers can help you find safe websites.

You may not be sure whether a website is safe for you to visit. You can always ask an adult you trust. He or she can help you find sites that are great for kids.

But even sites for kids can make mistakes. So check the information you learn with a parent, a teacher, or another trusted adult.

You can ask a teacher about things you read online.

Playing outside is a good way to spend time away from your computer.

It is also important to balance your computer time. Being on the computer all the time can be unhealthful. Be sure to take breaks to spend time with your family or to do other activities.

staying safe

Sticking to kid-friendly games and sites is one way to stay safe online. Another way is to keep your personal information private.

If you don't know what to keep private, just ask an adult for help.

Never give out your real name, age, address, or phone number online. Only adults should fill out forms that ask for this kind of information.

only adults should enter personal information online.

Don't include personal information in your usernames and passwords.

Think up usernames and passwords that only you can remember.

Avoid including things such as your name and birthday in usernames and passwords.

Login

Username

Password

Remember me ■

Forgot your password?

LOGIN

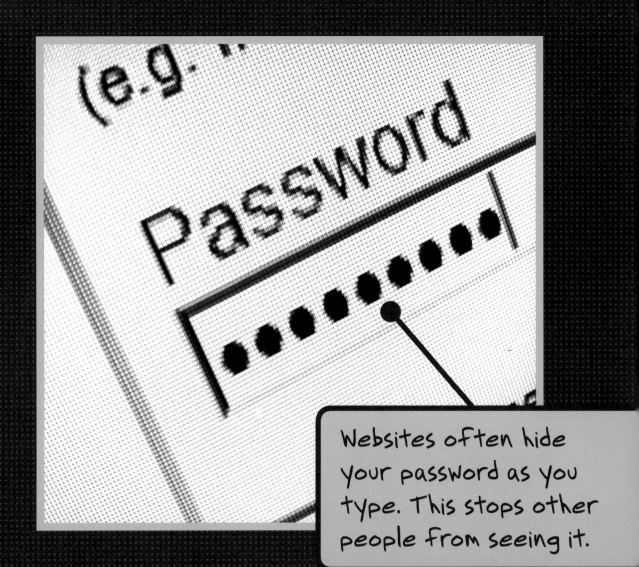

Websites often hide your password as you type. This stops other people from seeing it.

Mix uppercase letters with lowercase letters and numbers. This makes it harder for other people to guess your password.

Pretending to be another person is easy online.

It's easy to hide who you really are on the Internet. People online may not be who they say they are. Interact only with people you know and trust in real life.

You may see something online that seems wrong or feels uncomfortable. Be sure to tell an adult right away.

If you find something confusing online, always check with a trusted adult.

Showing Respect

When you are using a computer, it's important to respect yourself and others. Using good digital manners can help.

Manners online are just as important as manners in other places, such as the dinner table.

Think twice before you write or share any information. Whatever you put online leaves digital footprints that others can see.

Digital footprints are different from footprints in snow or sand. But just like real footprints, they leave a trail that others can see.

Together, your digital footprints create a picture of you. Make sure this picture reveals only what you want the world to know.

Digital footprints are like puzzle pieces that people can piece together to learn about you.

Picking on others online is known as cyberbullying. If you see cyberbullying online, tell an adult.

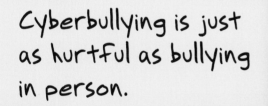

Cyberbullying is just as hurtful as bullying in person.

Always use respectful words online. If you want to share others' ideas or work, ask for their permission. Give them credit for their work.

If you see a cool picture online, you may want to use it yourself. But be sure to ask permission from its owner first.

If you use good manners, behave safely, and make wise choices, you will have great digital adventures!

Using computers safely can open the door to amazing virtual adventures.

Takeaway Tips

- Tell an adult when you use a computer. Ask an adult for help if needed.

- Keep your personal information private. Interact online only with people you know in real life. Tell an adult if something doesn't seem right.

- Leave a responsible digital footprint. Think twice before you share anything online.

- Treat people online the way you would like to be treated.

Fun Facts

- Researchers have found that taking breaks from using computers can help kids understand other people's feelings better.

- More than half of all American preschoolers have used a computer. Almost all American kids your age have.

- Your computer has a special number to identify it online. This number is like a phone number. It is called an Internet Protocol address (IP address). You leave a footprint of your IP address whenever you go online.

Glossary

citizen: a person who belongs to a community. Good citizens are safe, respectful, and make wise choices.

cyberbullying: being mean to others online

digital footprint: a record of your online activity

Internet: a network that connects computers all around the world

password: a secret series of numbers, letters, and symbols that lets only people who know it log in to a computer or a website

username: a series of numbers, letters, and symbols that identifies a computer user

website: a page on the Internet that contains information

Further Reading

Boothroyd, Jennifer. *From Chalkboards to Computers: How Schools Have Changed*. Minneapolis: Lerner Publications, 2012.

Boothroyd, Jennifer. *From Typewriters to Text Messages: How Communication Has Changed*. Minneapolis: Lerner Publications, 2012.

BrainPOP: Digital Etiquette
https://www.brainpop.com/technology/freemovies/digitaletiquette

Goldsmith, Mike. *Computer*. New York: DK, 2011.

PBS Kids: Webonauts Internet Academy
http://pbskids.org/webonauts

Index

Photo Acknowledgments

The images in this book are used with the permission of: © tmcphotos/Shutterstock Images, p. 2; © WavebreakMedia/Shutterstock Images, p. 4; © bogumil/Shutterstock Images, p. 5; © studerga/iStockphoto, p. 6; © Tyler Olson/Shutterstock Images, pp. 7, 14; © zerocreatives/Westend61/Corbis, p. 8; © shironosov/iStockphoto, p. 9; © fasphotographic/Shutterstock Images, p. 10; © Chepko Danil Vitalevich/Shutterstock Images, p. 11; © Pete Pahham/Shutterstock Images, p. 12; © Lisa F. Young/Shutterstock Images, p. 13; © Sergey Novikov/Shutterstock Images, p. 15; © Karen Struthers/Shutterstock Images, p. 16; © szefei/Shutterstock Images, p. 17; © Mixov/Shutterstock Images, p. 18; © isak55/Shutterstock Images, p. 19; © patrisyu/Shutterstock Images, p. 20; © Cathy Yeulet/Hemera/Thinkstock, p. 21; © 237/Robert Nicholas/Ocean/Corbis, p. 22; © Pavel L. Photo and Video/Shutterstock Images, p. 23; © vvoe/Shutterstock Images, p. 24; © stray cat/iStockphoto, p. 25; © Kamira/Shutterstock Images, p. 26; © Maridav/Shutterstock Images, p. 27; © Nicole Weiss/Shutterstock Images, p. 28; © Viacheslav Krylov/Shutterstock Images, p. 30; © Panom Pensawang/Shutterstock Images, p. 31.

Front cover: © iStockphoto.com/Christopher Futcher.

Main body text set in Johann light 30/36.